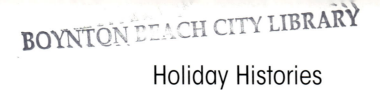
Holiday Histories

Presidents' Day

Mir Tamim Ansary

Heinemann Library
Chicago, Illinois

© 1999, 2006 Heinemann Library
a division of Reed Elsevier Inc.
Chicago, Illinois

Customer Service 888-454-2279
Visit our website at www.heinemannraintree.com

Designed by Kimberly Miracle and Q2A Creative
Printed in China by South China Printing Company

10 09 08 07 06
10 9 8 7 6 5 4 3 2 1

New edition ISBNs: 1-4034-8891-6 (hardcover)
                            1-4034-8904-1 (paperback)

The Library of Congress has cataloged the first edition as follows:
Ansary, Mir Tamim.
     Presidents' Day / Mir Tamim Ansary.
        p. cm. -- (Holiday histories)
     Includes bibliographical references and index.
     Summary: Introduces Presidents' Day, explaining the historical events behind it, how it became a holiday, and how it is observed.
     ISBN 1-57572-875-3 (lib. bdg.)
     1. Presidents' Day – Juvenile literature. 2. Presidents – United States – History – Juvenile literature.
     [1. Presidents' Day. 2. Presidents. 3. Holidays.] I. Title. II. Series: Ansary, Mir Tamim. Holiday histories.

E176.8 .A45 1998
394.261 – dc21
                                9814380

Acknowledgments
The author and publishers are grateful to the following for permission to reproduce photographs: AP/Wide World p. 24; Bettman Archive p. 16; Corbis-Bettmann p. 7; Getty Images pp. 28-29; The Granger Collection pp. 8, 10, 11, 12, 14, 20, 22, 23, 25 (top), 26; The Picture Cube, Inc. p. 4 (Kindra Clineff); Photo Researchers pp. 6 (Joe Sohm), 13 (Archive); SuperStock pp. 9, 15, 18, 21, 27.

Cover photograph reproduced with permission of Wally McNamee/Corbis.

Disclaimer
All the Internet addresses (URLs) given in this book were valid at the time of going to press. However, due to the dynamic nature of the Internet, some addresses may have changed, or sites may have changed or ceased to exist since publication. While the author and publisher regret any inconvenience this may cause readers, no responsibility for any such changes can be accepted by either the author or the publisher.

Contents

Some words are shown in bold, **like this**. You can find out what they mean by looking in the glossary.

A Winter Holiday

It is the middle of February. Christmas vacation ended long ago. Summer is still far away. Thank goodness for Presidents' Day!

4

This holiday is on the third Monday in February.
What a good time for a day off.

Honoring Our Leader

On Presidents' Day, we **honor** our country's leader. This person is chosen by the people. Every four years, adults vote for a new president.

The president lives in the White House, in Washington, D.C.

Sometimes they **elect** the same leader again.
But no one may be president more than twice.
Then someone else gets a turn.

Ronald Reagan, at left, became the 40th president in 1981.

How Presidents' Day Began

When your grandparents were born, Presidents' Day was not celebrated. In its place were two other holidays. Every state celebrated George Washington's birthday on February 22.

Many states also celebrated Abraham Lincoln's birthday. That falls on February 12. Washington was our first president and Lincoln was our sixteenth.

The Thirteen Colonies

Before Washington's time, the United States was not a country. It was a group of thirteen **colonies**. The **colonists** had come from Europe.

The leader of these colonies was the king of England. The colonists had to pay the king money. They had to obey his rules and his soldiers.

The American Revolution

The **colonists** got tired of this. They told the king they were a new country. The king did not agree. The Revolutionary War began.

George Washington led the American armies.
They won the Revolutionary War. The colonists
were free to set up a new country. But what kind?

A New Democracy

A long time ago, most countries had kings. Kings had total power. When they died, their sons almost always took over.

The Americans decided to try something new. They set up a democracy. In a democracy, the people have the power. They choose their own leaders.

Our First President

The people of the United States chose George Washington as their first leader. In fact, they **elected** him twice. Some people even asked him to be king.

Washington did something few people have done. He said no to power. He did not want to be president for a third time. This may have been one of his greatest deeds.

The Country Splits

Abraham Lincoln was **elected** president in 1860. This was a **tense** time. Some people in our country had **slaves**. Others wanted to end **slavery**.

The Southern states tried to split away from the
United States. Lincoln would not let them. He went
to war to stop the **rebels**. The Civil War began.

Why We Honor Lincoln

The Civil War lasted until 1865. It ended **slavery** in the United States. It gave this country a new start as a land of freedom.

We **honor** Lincoln for keeping the United States together. We honor him for helping to end slavery. Many Americans think he was our greatest president.

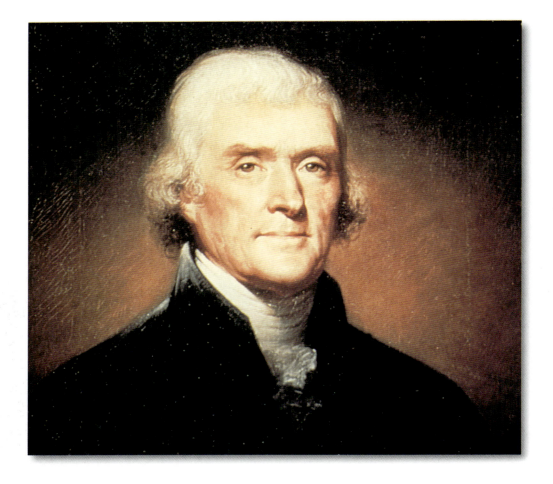

Jefferson and Wilson

There have been other great presidents.
There was Thomas Jefferson. He was our third
president. He helped to **found** our country.

There was Woodrow Wilson, our 28th president.
He led the United States through World War One.

Franklin D. Roosevelt

In 1930 much of the world became very poor. Many people lost their jobs. People stood in line for food. This time was called the Great **Depression**.

Our 32nd president helped end this depression.
Then he led our country through World War Two.
His name was Franklin D. Roosevelt.

Our Right to Choose Greatness

Our country **elected** 43 presidents in its first 218 years. Not all of them were perfect. Some are hardly even remembered.

William Henry Harrison
9th president

Millard Fillmore
13th president

Warren G. Harding
29th president

Presidents Washington, Jefferson, Theodore Roosevelt, and Lincoln are on the Mount Rushmore National Memorial in South Dakota.

But some of our presidents were truly great. They rose to power when they were needed most. Was this just luck? Probably not.

Celebrating Our Democracy

We the people chose the great presidents.
We **elected** the leaders we needed in times
of trouble. You may say we celebrate ourselves
on Presidents' Day.

We celebrate the fact that we have a president and not a king. We celebrate our democracy. That is why, on this day, we now **honor** all our presidents.

Important Dates

Presidents' Day

1607	First English **colony** is **founded** in North America
1775	The Revolutionary War begins
1776	American **colonists** declare their independence
1783	The Revolutionary War ends
1789–1797	George Washington is president of the United States
1801–1809	Thomas Jefferson is president
1861–1865	Abraham Lincoln is president
1913–1921	Woodrow Wilson is president
1929	The Great **Depression** begins
1933-1945	Franklin D. Roosevelt is president
1968	Presidents' Day replaces Washington's and Lincoln's birthdays

Glossary

colonies	land owned or controlled by another country
colonists	people who live in a colony
depression	time when most people are out of work and poor
elect	choose a leader
found	start something new
honor	show respect for someone
rebels	people who fight against their own government
slaves	people who were forced to work for other people and were owned, bought, and sold like property
slavery	use people as slaves
tense	full of worry

Find Out More

Burke, Rick. *Abraham Lincoln*. Chicago: Heinemann Library, 2003.
Burke, Rick. *George Washington*. Chicago: Heinemann Library, 2003.
Wade, Mary Dodson. *President's Day: Honoring the Birthdays of Washington and Lincoln*. Berkeley Heights, NJ: Enslow, 2004.

The White House Presidents' Day Page
http://www.whitehouse.gov/kids/presidentsday/

Index